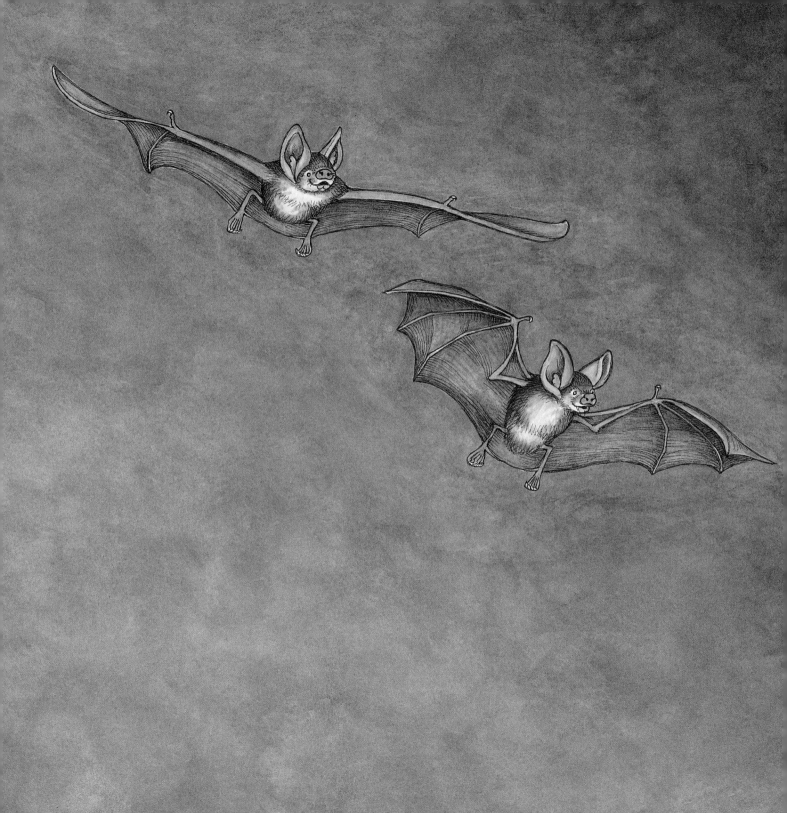

Hello,
Bumblebee Bat

Darrin Lunde

Illustrated by Patricia J. Wynne

ini Charlesbridge

Hello, little bat.
What is your name?

My name is Bumblebee Bat.

I am small, like a bee.

Bumblebee Bat, how small are you?

My body is one inch long.

I am six inches wide

when I spread my wings.

Bumblebee Bat, what do you look like?

My fur is reddish brown.

My nose looks like a pig's snout.

My ears are long and pointy.

My eyes are tiny specks.

Bumblebee Bat, when do you fly?

I fly before sunrise and just after dark.
I don't like bright sun.

Bumblebee Bat, how do you see at night?

I make a squeaky sound that
bounces back from whatever it hits.
I see by hearing.

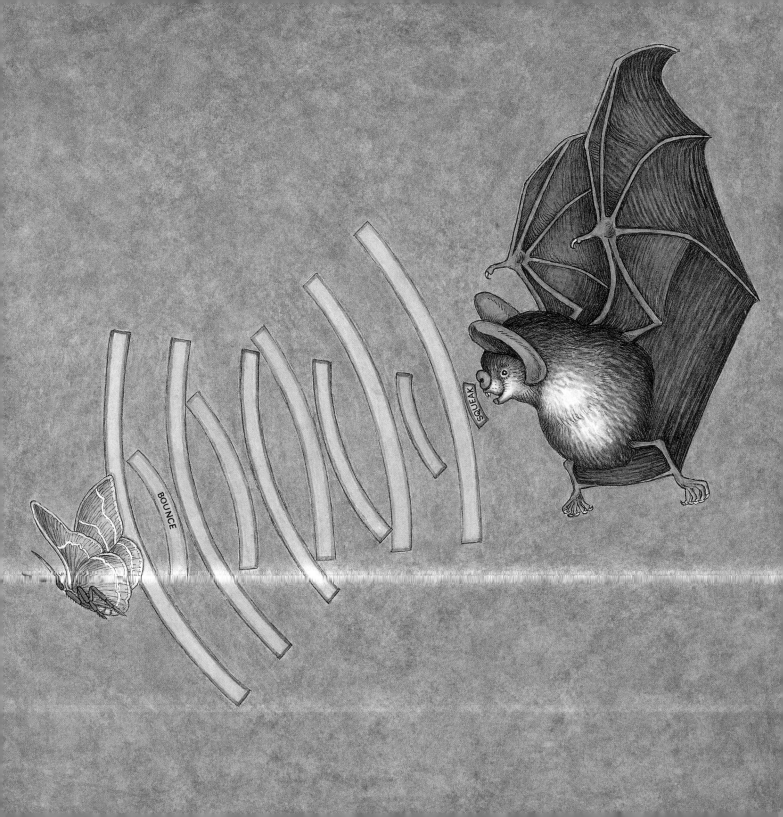

Bumblebee Bat, what do you eat?

I eat small insects like moths and flies.

Bumblebee Bat, what do you fear?

I am afraid of humans and birds.

Humans sometimes burn the forest
   near my home.

Birds try to eat me.

Bumblebee Bat, where do you live?

I live in a cave with my brothers and sisters.

Bumblebee Bat, how do you sleep?

I sleep hanging upside down in my cave.

I hold on with the sharp claws on my feet.

Good night,
Bumblebee Bat!

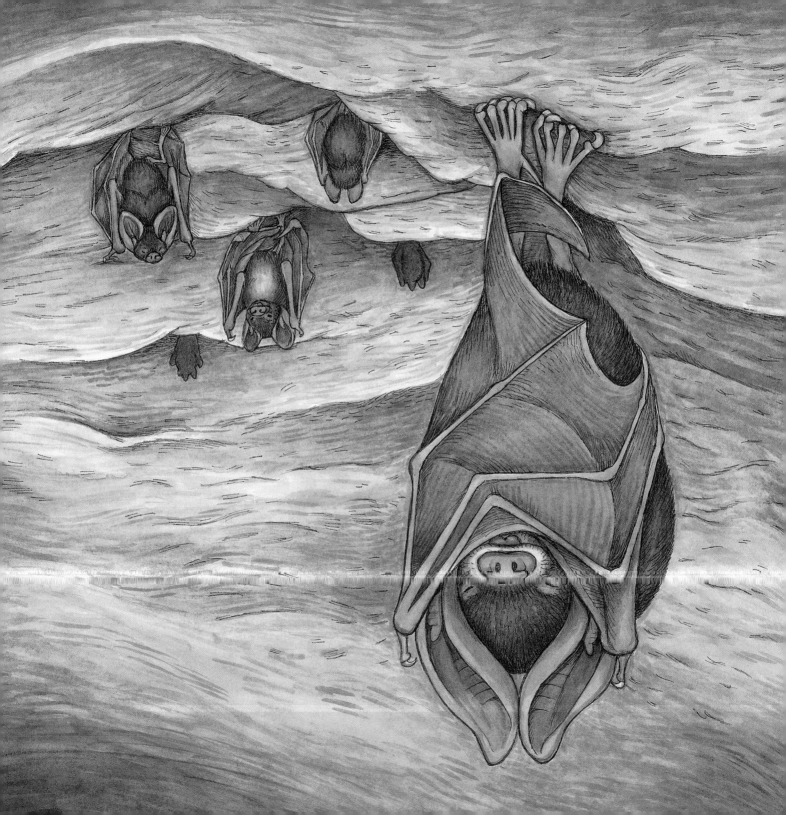

Bumblebee bats were discovered in western Thailand in 1973.

They are sometimes called Kitti's hog-nosed bats.

Bumblebee bats are the smallest bats in the world.

They are as light as a dime.

Bumblebee bats are very good at flying.

They can hover in one place for a short time.

Bumblebee bats are endangered.

This means they are very rare.

Bat scientists keep the location of the bats' caves secret.

This keeps the bats safe.

For my children: Sakura, Asahi, and little Midori—D. L.

For Maceo, another rare species—P. J. W.

Text copyright © 2007 by Darrin Lunde
Illustrations copyright © 2007 by Patricia J. Wynne

Published by Charlesbridge
85 Main Street
Watertown, MA 02472
(617) 926-0329
www.charlesbridge.com

Library of Congress Cataloging-in-Publication Data
Lunde, Darrin P.
    Hello, bumblebee bat / Darrin Lunde ; illustrated by Patricia J. Wynne.
        p. cm.
    ISBN 978-1-57091-374-7 (reinforced for library use)
    ISBN 978-1-57091-464-5 (softcover)
1. Bumblebee bat—Juvenile literature. I. Wynne, Patricia, ill. II. Title.
QL737.C513L86 2007
599.4—dc22   2006020952

Printed in China
(hc) 10 9 8 7 6 5 4 3
(sc) 10 9 8 7 6 5 4 3

Illustrations done in watercolor, ink, and colored pencil
Display type and text type set in Billy from SparkyType
Color separations by Chroma Graphics, Singapore
Printed and bound by Regent Publishing Services
Production supervision by Brian G. Walker
Designed by Susan Mallory Sherman

actual size